CW01511096

THE AUSTRALIAN
Women's Weekly

SUPER
KALE

CONTENTS

SMOOTHIES & SNACKS

KALE & BANANA SMOOTHIE

PREP TIME 5 MINUTES **SERVES** 4 (MAKES 1 LITRE)

- **2 medium ripe bananas (400g)**
- **2 cups (60g) shredded green kale leaves**
- **1 medium avocado (250g), chopped coarsely**
- **1½ tablespoons honey**
- **2 cups (500ml) water**
- **2 teaspoons linseeds**
- **crushed ice, to serve**

1 Place banana, kale, avocado, honey, the water and linseeds in a high-powered blender; blend until smooth.

2 Pour into glasses filled with crushed ice; serve immediately.

tips Wash the kale leaves, remove the stems before shredding the leaves. For a creamier smoothie, use frozen ripe bananas and have all the ingredients cold.

DAIRY-FREE • VEGAN • PALEO • HIGH-FIBRE

APPLE, KALE, AVOCADO & GINGER JUICE

PREP TIME 10 MINUTES SERVES 2

- 1 medium lime (90g)
- 1 medium apple (150g), chopped coarsely
- 1 lebanese cucumber (130g), chopped coarsely
- ½ medium avocado (125g), chopped coarsely
- 1⅓ cups (330ml) coconut water
- 30g (1 ounce) baby spinach leaves
- 1 teaspoon finely grated fresh ginger
- 50g (1½ ounces) baby kale leaves

1 Remove rind with pith from lime; discard. Coarsely chop lime flesh.

2 Blend or process lime and remaining ingredients until smooth. Divide juice between two glasses.

3 Serve immediately topped with crushed ice, if you like.

tips For smoothies it is best to use tender baby kale, that way you won't need to remove the hard stems. If you like, top the smoothies with chia seeds and toasted shredded coconut.

KALE CHIPS

PREP + COOK TIME 25 MINUTES (+ COOLING) SERVES 8

- **450g (14½ ounces) green kale leaves**
- **1 tablespoon extra virgin olive oil**
- **½ teaspoon crushed sea salt flakes**

1 Preheat oven to 190°C/375°F; place three large oven trays in the oven while preheating.

2 Remove and discard kale stems from leaves. Wash leaves well; pat dry with paper towel or in a salad spinner. Tear kale leaves into 5cm (2-inch) pieces; place in a large bowl, then drizzle with oil and sprinkle with salt. Using your hands, rub oil and salt through the kale. Spread kale, in a single layer, on warm trays.

3 Bake kale for 10 minutes. Remove any pieces of kale that are already crisp. Return remaining kale to the oven for a further 2 minutes; remove any pieces that are crisp. Repeat until all the kale is crisp. Cool.

tip These kale chips will keep in an airtight container for up to 2 weeks.

SUGAR-FREE • VEGAN • DAIRY-FREE • PALEO

GREEN SUPER JUICE

PREP TIME 5 MINUTES SERVES 3

- 1 lebanese cucumber, chopped coarsely
- 2 stalks celery (300g), trimmed, chopped coarsely
- 2 large green kale leaves (80g), trimmed, shredded coarsely
- 50g (1½ ounces) baby spinach leaves
- 1 medium green apple (150g), cored, chopped coarsely
- ½ lemon (70g), peeled
- 1 sprig fresh mint
- 1 cup (250ml) coconut water
- 1 cup ice cubes

1 Blend ingredients in a high-powered blender for 1 minute or until smooth. If required, stop the blender and push the ingredients down before blending again.

MAIN MEALS

KALE & SPINACH SPANAKOPITAS

PREP + COOK TIME 1 HOUR 30 MINUTES **MAKES** 6

- 1.5kg (3 pounds) silver beet (swiss chard)
- 350g (11 ounces) green kale leaves
- 400g (12½ ounces) greek fetta, crumbled
- 10 green onions (scallions), chopped finely
- ½ cup finely chopped fresh dill
- ¾ cup finely chopped fresh flat-leaf parsley
- 2 teaspoons finely grated lemon rind
- ¼ cup (60ml) lemon juice
- 3 eggs, beaten lightly
- 80g (2½ ounces) butter, melted
- 2 x 375g (12-ounce) packets fresh fillo pastry

1 Preheat oven to 180°C/350°F.

2 Trim 4cm (1½-inches) off the stalk ends from silver beet and kale; discard. Rinse and drain greens, leaving some water clinging. Tear kale leaves from the centre stem. Cut white stalk from silver beet leaves, cutting into the leaf in a v-shape. Finely chop stems and leaves from greens, keeping them separate.

3 Heat a large saucepan over high heat; cook stems, stirring occasionally, for 10 minutes or until softened. Drain well. Repeat with chopped leaves. When cool enough to handle, squeeze excess water from greens mixture.

4 Combine greens, fetta, onion, herbs, rind, juice, and eggs in a large bowl; season with freshly ground black pepper.

5 Butter six 2-cup (500ml), 12cm x 17cm (4¾-inch x 6¾-inch) oval oven dishes. Butter half a sheet of fillo pastry, fold in half to make a smaller rectangle; butter top. Place in dish, allowing pastry to overhang edge. Repeat with two more sheets of pastry, stacking them in the dish. You will now have six layers. Place a sixth of the filling into the tin. Brush half a sheet of fillo with melted butter, fold in half crossways, brush with butter, fold in half again; trim to fit the top of the pie. Place over filling, then fold in and scrunch the overhanging pastry. Brush top of pie with a little more melted butter. Repeat to make five more pies.

6 Sprinkle a little water over each pie. Bake for 45 minutes or until golden.

NUT-FREE • HIGH-FIBRE • RICH IN B-VITAMINS

ROASTED VEGIE PIZZA

PREP + COOK TIME 1 HOUR **SERVES** 2

- **100g (3 ounces) butternut pumpkin, sliced thinly**
- **cooking-oil spray**
- **2 teaspoons olive oil**
- **1 small brown onion (80g), chopped finely**
- **1 clove garlic, crushed**
- **250g (8 ounces) cherry tomatoes, quartered**
- **2 tablespoons finely chopped fresh basil leaves**
- **2 x 67g (2-ounce) wholemeal pita pockets**
- **1 small zucchini (90g), sliced into ribbons**
- **100g (3 ounces) green kale leaves, trimmed, shredded coarsely**
- **¼ cup (60g) reduced-fat ricotta, crumbled**
- **1½ tablespoons pine nuts, toasted**
- **2 tablespoons small basil leaves, extra**

1 Preheat oven to 200°C/400°F. Line two oven trays with baking paper.

2 Place pumpkin on one tray; spray with cooking oil. Bake for 20 minutes or until softened.

3 Heat oil in a medium saucepan over medium heat; cook onion and garlic, stirring, for 4 minutes or until softened. Add tomato; stir to combine. Bring to the boil, then reduce heat to low; simmer, uncovered, for 10 minutes or until mixture is thickened. Stir in the basil.

4 Arrange pita pockets on remaining oven tray. Spread with tomato mixture; top with pumpkin, zucchini and kale. Bake for 15 minutes or until bases are crisp.

5 Top pizzas with ricotta, nuts and extra basil before serving. Season with pepper.

tip Use a vegetable peeler, mandoline or V-slicer to slice the zucchini into ribbons.

19

LAMB, HALOUMI & KALE SALAD WITH CHIMICHURRI DRESSING

PREP + COOK TIME 40 MINUTES SERVES 6

- **600g (1¼ pound) lamb rump steaks, trimmed**
- **2 teaspoons olive oil**
- **1 small red onion (120g), sliced thinly**
- **2 cups (60g) thickly sliced trimmed kale leaves**
- **250g (8 ounces) haloumi, sliced thickly**
- **2 small tomatoes (180g), seeded, sliced thinly**
- **200g (6½-ounce) packet crunchy combo sprout mix**

CHIMICHURRI DRESSING

- **1 cup coarsely chopped fresh flat-leaf parsley**
- **2 tablespoons coarsely chopped fresh oregano**
- **2 cloves garlic, crushed**
- **1 tablespoon red wine vinegar**
- **2 tablespoons lemon juice**
- **½ cup (125ml) extra virgin olive oil**

1 Make chimichurri dressing.

2 Cook lamb on a heated, oiled grill pan (or grill or barbecue) for 4 minutes each side or until cooked as desired. Transfer to a plate; cover tightly with foil, rest for 5 minutes. Slice lamb into 5mm (¼-inch) slices.

3 Meanwhile, heat oil in a large frying pan; cook onion, stirring, for 5 minutes or until just softened. Add kale; cook, stirring, for 2 minutes until kale changes colour and softens slightly. Transfer to a large bowl.

4 Cook haloumi in same pan, over medium heat, for 1 minute each side or until browned and just melting.

5 Add lamb and haloumi to kale mixture, with tomato and sprouts; toss gently to combine. Serve salad drizzled with chimichurri dressing.

CHIMICHURRI DRESSING

Combine ingredients in a bowl.

tip Any leftover chimichurri can be stored in an airtight container in the fridge for up to 2 weeks.

GLUTEN-FREE • EGG-FREE • NUT-FREE

HIGH IN VITAMIN A & K · LACTO-VEGETARIAN

KUMARA SOUP WITH KALE CHIPS

PREP + COOK TIME 35 MINUTES **SERVES** 4

- 2 tablespoons extra virgin olive oil
- 1 medium brown onion (150g), chopped coarsely
- 2 cloves garlic, crushed
- 1 teaspoon ground cumin
- pinch mexican chilli powder
- 600g (1¼ pounds) kumara (orange sweet potato), chopped coarsely
- 2 medium potatoes (400g), chopped coarsely
- 2 cups (500ml) water
- 1½ cups (375ml) vegetable stock
- ½ cup (125ml) pouring cream
- 1 tablespoon lemon juice

KALE CHIPS

- 200g (6½ ounces) green kale leaves
- 1 tablespoon extra virgin olive oil
- ½ teaspoon crushed sea salt flakes

1 Heat half the oil in a large saucepan over medium-high heat; cook onion and garlic, stirring, for 5 minutes or until onion softens. Add spices; cook, stirring, for 1 minute or until fragrant. Add kumara, potato, the water and stock; bring to the boil. Reduce heat; simmer, covered, for 20 minutes or until vegetables are tender. Cool soup for 10 minutes.

2 Meanwhile, make kale chips.

3 Blend or process soup, in batches, until smooth. Return soup to same pan; add cream and juice. Reheat, stirring, without boiling, until hot. Season to taste.

4 Serve bowls of soup topped with kale chips; drizzle with remaining oil.

KALE CHIPS Preheat oven to 190°C/375°F. Place a large oven tray in the oven while preheating. Strip kale from stems. Wash kale well; pat dry with paper towel or in a salad spinner. Tear kale leaves into 5cm (2-inch) pieces; place in a large bowl, then drizzle with oil and sprinkle with salt. Rub salt and oil through the kale. Spread kale in a single layer on tray. Bake for 10 minutes. Remove pieces of kale that are crisp. Bake remaining kale for a further 2 minutes then remove crisp pieces. Repeat until all the kale is crisp. Cool.

tip You need about half a bunch of kale for this recipe.

WHOLEMEAL PASTA WITH KALE & WALNUT PESTO

PREP + COOK TIME 20 MINUTES **SERVES** 4

- 2 cups (60g) coarsely chopped green kale leaves
- ½ cup loosely packed fresh flat-leaf parsley leaves
- 1 cup (80g) finely grated parmesan
- ¼ cup (60ml) lemon juice
- 2 tablespoons roasted walnuts
- 1 cup (250ml) extra virgin olive oil
- 400g (12½ ounces) wholemeal spaghetti or short tubular pasta
- pinch chilli flakes

1 Process kale with parsley, parmesan, juice, walnuts and oil until almost smooth. Season.

2 Cook pasta in a large saucepan of boiling salted water until almost tender; drain, reserving ¼ cup of the cooking liquid.

3 Return pasta to pan, off the heat. Add pesto and reserved cooking liquid; toss gently to combine. Serve topped with chilli flakes.

VEGETARIAN•HIGH IN HEALTHY FATS•VITAMIN-RICH•

SAUSAGE, KALE & EGGS

PREP + COOK TIME 1 HOUR **SERVES** 6

- **2 large dutch cream potatoes (600g), quartered lengthways**
- **1 medium kumara (orange sweet potato) (400g), quartered lengthways**
- **1.2kg (2½ pounds) good-quality gluten-free pork and fennel sausages**
- **¼ cup (60ml) olive oil**
- **250g (8 ounces) green kale, trimmed, torn roughly**
- **2 cloves garlic, crushed**
- **¾ cup (210g) tomato paste**
- **2 cups (500ml) hot water**
- **½ teaspoon cayenne pepper**
- **6 eggs**

1 Cook potato and kumara in a large saucepan of boiling water for 20 minutes or until tender. Drain; season to taste. Wash pan; dry.

2 Meanwhile, squeeze sausage meat from skins; discard skins. Using damp hands, form sausage meat into walnut-sized roughly shaped balls; place on a baking-paper-lined tray. Cover; refrigerate until required.

3 Return same large saucepan to medium heat with 1 tablespoon of the oil; cook kale, stirring, for 3 minutes or until bright green. Drain on paper towel.

4 Add half the remaining oil to same pan; cook sausage meat, in batches, turning occasionally, for 4 minutes or until browned. (If the sausage meat starts to stick to the pan, stir in 1 tablespoon water to release it from the base.)

5 Return all sausage meat to pan; reduce heat to low. Add garlic; stir for 1 minute or until fragrant. Add potato and kumara; stir gently until just combined. Combine tomato paste, the water and cayenne pepper in a medium jug.

Increase heat to high. Stir in tomato paste mixture; bring to the boil. Reduce heat to low; cook, covered, for 5 minutes. Stir in kale until heated through; season to taste.

6 Meanwhile, heat remaining oil in a large non-stick frying pan over medium heat. Fry eggs, in two batches, until cooked as desired. Season.

7 Serve sausage and kale mixture in individual bowls topped with fried egg.

tips You may need to clean the saucepan in between cooking each batch of sausage meat. Also, try not to stir the sausage meat too often, as it will brown better and cook faster if left undisturbed. This dish is a great way to use up your leftover vegetables. This recipe is best made close to serving.

LAZY KALE TORTILLA

PREP + COOK TIME 30 MINUTES SERVES 4

- **3 cups (90g) torn green kale leaves**
- **1 cup loosely packed fresh flat-leaf parsley leaves**
- **1 cup loosely packed fresh dill sprigs**
- **3 green onions (scallions), halved**
- **9 eggs**
- **2 slices wholemeal bread (90g), torn**
- **¼ cup (60ml) olive oil**
- **¼ cup loosely packed fresh flat-leaf parsley, extra**
- **1 medium lemon (140g), cut into wedges**

1 Preheat oven to 200°C/400°F.

2 Pulse kale in a food processor until coarsely chopped; transfer to a bowl. Repeat with parsley, dill and onion; transfer to bowl.

3 Add eggs and bread; mix to combine. Season.

4 Heat a 26cm (10½ inch) ovenproof frying pan over medium heat. When pan is hot, add 2 tablespoons of the oil then egg mixture; cook for 8 minutes or until tortilla is three-quarters set.

5 Transfer to oven; cook a further 15 minutes or until set. Serve drizzled with remaining olive oil, sprinkle with extra parsley; accompany with lemon wedges.

VEGETARIAN • PROTEIN-RICH • HIGH IN VITAMIN B6 • OVO-

ROASTED KALE & GRILLED CHICKEN SALAD

PREP + COOK TIME 50 MINUTES SERVES 4

- **350g (11 ounces) green kale leaves**
- **¼ cup (60ml) olive oil**
- **400g (12½ ounces) baby (dutch) carrots, trimmed, halved lengthways**
- **400g (12½ ounces) chicken breast fillets**
- **½ small red onion (50g), sliced thinly**
- **½ cup loosely packed small fresh flat-leaf parsley leaves**
- **2 tablespoons pepitas (pumpkin seeds), roasted**

LEMON DRESSING

- **⅓ cup (100g) whole-egg mayonnaise**
- **1 teaspoon finely grated lemon rind**
- **2 tablespoons lemon juice**
- **2 teaspoons dijon mustard**
- **1 small clove garlic, crushed**

1 Preheat oven to 180°C/350°F. Line three oven trays with baking paper.

2 Cut leaves from kale; discard stems. Place kale on two trays; drizzle with 1 tablespoon of the oil. Place carrots on remaining tray; drizzle with half the remaining oil. Roast carrots for 30 minutes or until tender, adding kale to oven for the last 10 minutes of cooking time or until kale is crisp.

3 Meanwhile, cut chicken fillets in half horizontally to form four thin fillets; drizzle with remaining oil. Cook chicken on heated lightly oiled grill plate (or grill or barbecue) until browned and cooked through; slice thickly.

4 Make lemon dressing.

5 Place kale, carrot, onion, chicken, dressing and half the parsley in a large bowl; toss to combine. Serve topped with remaining parsley and pepitas.

LEMON DRESSING

Combine ingredients in a small bowl; season to taste.

tips You will need 1 bunch of kale. For a vegetarian option, you can omit the chicken and step 3. Add two 400g (12½-ounce) cans drained, rinsed chickpeas (garbanzo beans) to oven tray with the carrots in step 2.

31

RED RICE & KALE SALAD

PREP + COOK TIME 50 MINUTES SERVES 2

- 1 cup (200g) red rice
- 1 cup (240g) frozen peas
- 250g (8 ounces) green beans, trimmed, chopped coarsely
- 150g (4½ ounces) purple kale leaves, trimmed, chopped coarsely
- 2 tablespoons olive oil
- 1½ teaspoons dijon mustard
- 1 tablespoon white wine vinegar
- 2½ tablespoons olive oil, extra
- 100g (3 ounces) fetta, crumbled

1 Preheat oven to 200°C/400°F.

2 Cook rice in a medium saucepan of boiling water for 35 minutes. Add peas and beans; cook for a further 5 minutes or until rice and vegetables are tender; drain. Rinse under cold water; drain.

3 Meanwhile, toss kale with oil on a baking-paper-lined oven tray; season. Roast 10 minutes or until crisp.

4 Whisk mustard, vinegar and extra oil in a medium bowl until combined; season. Add rice mixture and half the kale; toss to combine.

5 Serve salad topped with remaining kale and fetta.

HIGH-FIBRE • GLUTEN-FREE • VEGETARIAN •

KALE, CHILLI & PARMESAN PASTA

PREP + COOK TIME 20 MINUTES   SERVES 4

- 2 cups (60g) coarsely chopped green kale leaves
- 2 cups (160g) finely grated parmesan
- 1 cup firmly packed fresh flat-leaf parsley leaves
- 2 cloves garlic, crushed
- 1 tablespoon finely grated lemon rind
- ⅔ cup (160ml) lemon juice
- 1 cup (250ml) extra virgin olive oil, plus extra for drizzling
- 1 cup (120g) sourdough, torn coarsely
- 500g (1 pound) spelt or wholemeal spaghettini
- pinch dried chilli flakes

1 To make kale pesto, process kale, parmesan, parsley, garlic, rind, half the juice and ⅔ cup of the oil until smooth; season to taste.

2 Heat remaining oil in a large frying pan over medium-high heat; add sourdough, stir for 2 minutes or until lightly golden. Transfer to a plate lined with paper towel.

3 Cook pasta in a large saucepan of boiling water until almost tender. Reserve 2 tablespoons of the cooking water then drain pasta. Return pasta to pan with reserved cooking water; stir in kale pesto and remaining juice. Season to taste.

4 Serve pasta topped with toasted sourdough, chilli flakes, and extra parmesan, if you like.

tips This is a great way to use up leafy greens and herbs. For the pesto, try substituting basil or mint for the parsley, and rocket or baby spinach for the kale. You could also use baby kale leaves that is sold in packets from the supermarket.

HIGH IN VITAMIN C·VEGETARIAN·HIGH·FIBRE·HIGH IN

QUINOA, KALE & CORIANDER SALAD

PREP + COOK TIME 40 MINUTES **SERVES** 4

- 1 cup (200g) tri-colour quinoa
- 2 cups (500ml) water
- 450g (14½ ounces) broccolini, trimmed, halved crossways
- 280g (9 ounces) green kale leaves, trimmed, torn coarsely
- ¼ cup (50g) pepitas (pumpkin seeds)
- ⅓ cup (55g) coarsely chopped smoked almonds
- 2 fresh long green chillies, seeded, sliced thinly
- 3 cloves garlic, chopped finely
- ¼ cup (60ml) extra virgin olive oil
- 1 large avocado (320g), chopped coarsely

CORIANDER DRESSING

- 1 cup loosely packed fresh coriander (cilantro) leaves
- 1 fresh long green chilli, seeded, chopped
- ¼ cup (60ml) olive oil
- 2 tablespoons lime juice

1 Preheat oven to 220°C/425°F.

2 Place quinoa and the water in a medium saucepan; bring to the boil. Reduce heat to low; simmer, covered, for 10 minutes or until tender. Rinse under cold water; drain well. Transfer quinoa to a large bowl.

3 Combine broccolini, kale, pepitas, almonds, chilli, garlic and oil in a large shallow baking dish or baking trays; season. Roast for 8 minutes or until broccoli is tender and kale is wilted, stirring the mixture twice during cooking.

4 Meanwhile, make coriander dressing.

5 Add kale mixture to quinoa; toss gently to combine. Serve salad topped with avocado, drizzled with dressing.

CORIANDER DRESSING

Place ingredients in a blender or food processor; pulse until finely chopped. Season to taste.

tips Cauliflower is also delicious roasted in the same way; allow an extra 10 minutes cooking time. Squeeze a little extra lime juice over the avocado to prevent browning if you are packaging and transporting the salad.

HIGH-FIBRE • FOLATE & PROTEIN-RICH

SUGAR-FREE • HIGH-FIBRE • PROTEIN-RICH

POACHED EGGS & KALE PESTO SALAD

PREP + COOK TIME 25 MINUTES **SERVES** 2

- ¾ cup (45g) firmly packed baby leaf micro herb mix
- 100g (3 ounces) brussels sprouts, shaved thinly
- 1 cup (150g) crunchy combo sprout mix
- 1 small carrot (80g), cut into matchsticks
- 2 tablespoons toasted sunflower seeds
- 2 tablespoons apple cider vinegar
- 1½ tablespoons avocado oil
- 1 teaspoon raw honey
- 1 tablespoon white vinegar
- 4 eggs
- ½ medium avocado (125g), sliced thinly

KALE PESTO

- ⅓ cup (55g) dry-roasted almonds
- ⅓ cup (50g) roasted cashews
- 2 small cloves garlic
- 2 cups (80g) baby kale leaves, chopped coarsely
- ½ cup (125ml) extra virgin olive oil
- 1½ tablespoons apple cider vinegar
- ¼ cup (20g) finely grated parmesan

1 Make kale pesto.

2 Place baby leaves, brussels sprouts, sprout mix, carrot and seeds in a medium bowl; toss to combine. Whisk cider vinegar, 1 tablespoon of the oil and honey in a small bowl; season to taste. Add dressing to salad; toss to combine.

3 To poach eggs, half-fill a large, deep-frying pan with water, add white vinegar; bring to a gentle simmer. Break 1 egg into a cup. Using a wooden spoon, make a whirlpool in the water; slide egg into whirlpool. Repeat with 3 more eggs. Cook eggs for 3 minutes or until whites are set and the yolks are runny. Remove eggs with a slotted spoon; drain on a paper-towel-lined plate.

4 Divide salad between serving bowls; top with eggs and avocado. Spoon pesto on eggs; drizzle with remaining oil.

KALE PESTO Pulse nuts and garlic in a food processor until coarsely chopped. Add kale, oil and vinegar; pulse to a fine paste. Add parmesan, season; pulse until just combined. (Makes 1¼ cups)

RAW KALE & BROCCOLI SALAD

PREP TIME 20 MINUTES SERVES 2

- 350g (11 ounces) broccoli, cut into medium-sized florets
- 1 medium pear (230g), cored, quartered
- 2 cups (80g) firmly packed coarsely chopped purple kale leaves
- 2 teaspoons tamarind puree
- 2 tablespoons tamari
- 1 tablespoon lime juice
- 2 teaspoons sesame oil
- 2 tablespoons sesame seeds

1 Using a mandoline or V-slicer, cut broccoli florets and pear quarters into thin slices.

2 Arrange kale, broccoli and pear on a serving platter. Combine tamarind puree, tamari, juice, oil and sesame seeds in a jug; drizzle over salad.

40

GREEN SHAKSHUKA

PREP + COOK TIME 30 MINUTES SERVES 4

- **2 tablespoons olive oil**
- **1 medium leek (350g), sliced thinly**
- **1 clove garlic, sliced thinly**
- **1 baby fennel bulb (130g), trimmed, sliced thinly, fronds reserved**
- **150g (4½ ounces) green kale leaves, trimmed, chopped coarsely**
- **½ cup (125ml) vegetable stock**
- **8 eggs**
- **½ cup (125g) drained labne**
- **¼ cup (60g) halved spicy green olives**
- **¼ teaspoon ground sumac**
- **4 pitta pocket bread (150g)**

1 Heat oil in a large frying pan over medium heat; cook leek, garlic, fennel and kale, stirring occasionally, for 5 minutes or until vegetables soften. Stir in stock; bring to a simmer.

2 Using the back of a spoon, make eight shallow indents in the mixture. Break 1 egg into each hole. Cook, covered, over low heat, for 6 minutes or until egg whites are set and yolks remain runny, or until cooked to your liking. Season.

3 Top shakshuka with labne and olives; sprinkle with sumac and reserved fennel fronds. Serve with char-grilled pitta bread.

tip You can use silver beet (swiss chard) or spinach instead of the kale, if you prefer.

LACTO-OVO VEGETARIAN · PROTEIN-RICH ·

43

PORK, SOPRESSA & KALE PESTO PASTA

PREP + COOK TIME 30 MINUTES SERVES 4

- ½ cup (125ml) olive oil
- 600g (1¼ pounds) pork fillets
- 375g (12 ounces) casarecci pasta
- 1 medium brown onion (150g), chopped finely
- 2 cloves garlic, crushed
- 100g (3 ounces) hot sopressa salami, sliced thinly
- 100g (3 ounces) baby kale leaves
- ¼ cup (20g) finely grated parmesan
- 1 tablespoon roasted pine nuts
- 2 tablespoons lemon juice
- ½ cup micro basil leaves

1 Heat 1 tablespoon of the oil in a large frying pan over medium-high heat; cook pork, turning, for 15 minutes or until cooked. Remove pork from pan; cover to keep warm.

2 Meanwhile, cook pasta in a large saucepan of boiling salted water about 8 minutes or until tender; drain. Return to pan to keep warm.

3 Cook onion, garlic and salami in same frying pan, stirring, for 5 minutes or until onion softens.

4 Blend or process kale, remaining oil, parmesan, nuts and juice until smooth; season.

5 Thinly slice pork. Add pork, salami mixture and kale pesto to pasta in pan; toss to combine. Serve sprinkled with basil leaves.

tip Sopressa, a salami from the north of Italy, can be found in both mild and chilli-flavoured varieties. If unavailable, you can use any hot salami.

WINTER VEGIE BOWL

PREP + COOK TIME 40 MINUTES SERVES 4

- 800g (1½ pounds) jap pumpkin, unpeeled, cut into thin wedges
- 2 tablespoons olive oil
- 4 eggs
- 450g (14½ ounces) packaged microwave brown rice
- 120g (4 ounces) green kale, trimmed
- 160g (5 ounces) mild blue cheese, cut into 4 wedges
- ½ cup (50g) roasted walnuts, chopped coarsely
- 2 tablespoons pepitas (pumpkin seeds), toasted
- 2 teaspoons linseeds, toasted

PARSLEY DRESSING

- 1 shallot (25g), chopped finely
- 2 tablespoons finely chopped fresh flat-leaf parsley
- 1 clove garlic, crushed
- 1 tablespoon dijon mustard
- ¼ cup (60ml) olive oil
- ⅓ cup (80ml) white wine vinegar

1 Preheat oven to 200°C/400°F. Line a large oven tray with baking paper.

2 Place pumpkin wedges on tray; drizzle with oil. Season. Roast for 30 minutes or until tender and golden.

3 Meanwhile, place eggs in a saucepan of cold water. Bring to the boil; boil eggs for 4 minutes. Drain. Place eggs under cold running water until cool enough to handle. Peel eggs; halve lengthways.

4 Make parsley dressing.

5 Heat rice according to packet instructions.

6 Thinly slice kale leaves; place in a large bowl with half the dressing. Using your hands, gently massage dressing into kale to soften the leaves.

7 Place kale and rice in serving bowls; top with pumpkin, eggs and cheese. Sprinkle with walnuts and seeds; drizzle with remaining dressing.

PARSLEY DRESSING

Combine ingredients in a small bowl. Season to taste.

tip Recipe can be prepared ahead of time; add the dressing just before serving.

CAULIFLOWER, KALE & CHICKPEA CURRY

PREP + COOK TIME 40 MINUTES SERVES 4

- 2 tablespoons olive oil
- 1 medium brown onion (150g), sliced thickly
- 1 large red capsicum (bell pepper) (350g), sliced thickly
- 1 clove garlic, crushed
- 2 teaspoons finely grated fresh ginger
- 2 fresh small red thai chillies, chopped finely
- 1 teaspoon ground cumin
- ½ teaspoon ground turmeric
- ¼ teaspoon ground cardamom
- ¼ teaspoon ground fennel
- 1 small cauliflower (1kg), trimmed, sliced thickly
- 400g (12½ ounces) canned diced tomatoes
- 400ml canned coconut cream
- 1 cup (250ml) vegetable stock
- 1 tablespoon tomato paste
- 175g (5½ ounces) chopped green kale leaves
- 400g (12½ ounces) canned chickpeas (garbanzo beans), drained, rinsed
- ½ cup loosely packed fresh small mint leaves

1 Heat oil in a large saucepan over medium-high heat; cook onion, capsicum, garlic, ginger and chilli, stirring, for 5 minutes or until onion softens. Add spices and cauliflower; cook, stirring, for 2 minutes.

2 Add tomatoes, coconut cream, stock and paste; bring to the boil. Reduce heat; simmer, uncovered, for 20 minutes. Add kale and chickpeas; simmer, uncovered, about 10 minutes or until vegetables are tender. Season.

3 Serve bowls of curry sprinkled with mint.

serving suggestion Serve with steamed jasmine rice.

NUT-FREE • VEGAN • DAIRY-FREE • VITAMIN C-RICH

SALAD OF CRUNCHY THINGS

PREP + COOK TIME 20 MINUTES **SERVES** 4

- ⅓ cup **(80ml) extra virgin olive oil**
- **2 tablespoons sesame seeds**
- **2 tablespoons sunflower seeds**
- **2 tablespoons pepitas (pumpkin seeds)**
- **2 teaspoons chia seeds**
- **1 tablespoon tamari**
- **2 medium kohlrabi (1kg), trimmed**
- **400g (12½ ounces) brussels sprouts**
- **4 medium purple kale leaves (120g), trimmed**
- **¾ cup loosely packed fresh flat-leaf parsley leaves**
- **2 tablespoons lemon juice**
- **1 clove garlic, crushed**
- **2 teaspoons dijon mustard**

1 Stir 1 tablespoon of the oil, sesame seeds, sunflower seeds and pepitas in a small frying pan, over medium heat, for 5 minutes or until golden. Add chia seeds and tamari; stir to combine.

2 Using the shredder attachment on a food processor, grate kohlrabi and brussels sprouts. Tip vegetables into a large bowl. Process kale leaves until chopped coarsely; add to bowl with parsley.

3 Process remaining oil with juice, garlic and mustard until combined; season to taste. Toss vegetables with dressing; top with seed mixture.

GLUTEN-FREE • HIGH-FIBRE • PROTEIN-RICH • VEGAN

KALE CAESAR SALAD WITH CHICKPEA CROÛTONS

PREP + COOK TIME 20 MINUTES SERVES 4

- 4 eggs
- 500g (1 pound) green kale leaves, trimmed, chopped coarsely
- 1 tablespoon olive oil
- ½ teaspoon sea salt
- ½ cup (40g) shaved parmesan
- micro radish leaves, to serve

CHICKPEA CROÛTONS

- 400g (12½ ounces) canned chickpeas (garbanzo beans), drained, rinsed
- 1 tablespoon olive oil
- 1 teaspoon smoked paprika
- ¼ cup (40g) smoked almonds, chopped coarsely

BUTTERMILK DRESSING

- ⅓ cup (80ml) buttermilk
- 2 teaspoons lemon juice
- 1 teaspoon dijon mustard
- 1 large anchovy fillet, chopped finely
- ½ clove garlic, crushed

1 Make chickpea croûtons.

2 Meanwhile, place eggs in a medium saucepan with enough cold water to cover; bring to the boil. Reduce heat; simmer, uncovered, for 4 minutes for soft boiled. Drain; refresh under cold running water. Peel eggs.

3 Make buttermilk dressing.

4 Place kale, oil and salt in a large bowl; rub well to soften the leaves, it will lose about half its volume. Add chickpea croûtons and half the dressing; toss gently to combine.

5 Serve topped with halved eggs, parmesan, micro leaves and remaining dressing.

CHICKPEA CROÛTONS
Combine ingredients in a medium bowl. Cook chickpea mixture in a large frying pan over high heat, stirring, for 8 minutes, or until crisp. Cool.

BUTTERMILK DRESSING
Place ingredients in a screw-top jar; shake well.

tip You could use baby kale leaves if you prefer, as they are not as tough as regular kale.

serving suggestion Add some sliced smoked chicken.

HIGH GI · LOW · IRON · VITAMIN A-RICH

BROWN RICE & KALE STIR-FRY

PREP + COOK TIME 15 MINUTES **SERVES** 2

- **100g (3 ounces) green kale leaves**
- **1 medium brown onion (150g), chopped coarsely**
- **cooking-oil spray**
- **1 cup (165g) cooked brown rice**
- **1 teaspoon grated fresh ginger**
- **2 teaspoons salt-reduced soy sauce**
- **2 eggs**
- **½ fresh long red chilli, sliced thinly**
- **2 teaspoons toasted sesame seeds**

1 Coarsely chop the kale stalks and leaves.

2 Lightly spray a large non-stick frying pan with oil; cook onion and kale stalks, over medium heat, for 3 minutes. Stir in kale leaves, rice, ginger and sauce; cook until hot. Transfer to a large bowl; cover to keep warm.

3 Wipe pan clean. Lightly spray with oil; cook eggs, over low heat, until cooked as desired.

4 Serve rice topped with eggs. Sprinkle with chilli slices and sesame seeds.

PARSNIP SOUP WITH KALE CHIPS

PREP + COOK TIME 1 HOUR 20 MINUTES (+ STANDING) SERVES 8

- 2kg (4 pounds) parsnips, chopped coarsely
- 2 medium brown onions (300g), chopped coarsely
- 1 stalk celery (150g), trimmed
- 3 cloves garlic, quartered
- 1.5 litres (6 cups) water
- 1 litre (4 cups) chicken or vegetable stock
- ⅓ cup (80ml) olive oil
- 6 cloves garlic, extra, bruised
- ½ cup (125ml) pouring cream
- 2 tablespoons lemon juice

KALE CHIPS

- 200g (6½ ounces) green kale leaves, washed, dried
- 1 clove garlic, crushed
- 2 tablespoons extra virgin olive oil
- 2 tablespoons dukkah

1 Place parsnip, onion, celery, quartered garlic, the water and stock in a large saucepan; bring to the boil. Reduce heat; simmer, covered, for 1 hour or until tender. Remove pan from heat; cool, uncovered, for 10 minutes.

2 Meanwhile, heat oil with extra garlic in a small saucepan over medium heat. When oil begins to sizzle; remove pan from heat. Cool. When cool, discard garlic.

3 Meanwhile, make kale chips.

4 Blend or process soup, in batches, until smooth. Return soup to pan; stir in cream, over medium-high heat, until hot. Season. Stir in juice.

5 Serve soup drizzled with garlic oil and topped with kale chips.

KALE CHIPS Preheat oven to 220°C/425°F. Tear the leafy part of the kale from stalks then tear into 3cm (1½-inch) pieces. Discard stalks. Place kale on two large oven trays lined with baking paper. Combine garlic and oil; drizzle half over each tray of kale, then toss well to combine. Spread kale out in a single layer. Bake for 8 minutes, turning kale and swapping trays from top to bottom, halfway through cooking time, or until kale is crisp. Season with salt; sprinkle with dukkah.

tips Be extremely careful when blending hot soup – let it cool a little first. Don't over-fill the blender, one-third to half-full is a good guide, and make sure the lid is secure. Alternatively, use a stick blender.

HIGH-FIBRE • HIGH IN VITAMIN C

BROCCOLI & KALE SOUP WITH LEMON CRÈME FRAÎCHE

PREP + COOK TIME 30 MINUTES SERVES 4

- 200g (6½ ounces) green kale leaves, trimmed, chopped coarsely
- 1½ tablespoons olive oil
- 1 large brown onion (200g), chopped finely
- 3 cloves garlic, chopped finely
- 1.5 litres (6 cups) vegetable stock
- 650g (1¼ pounds) sebago potatoes, chopped coarsely
- 450g (14½ ounces) broccoli, cut into florets, stems sliced thinly
- 1 cup loosely packed fresh flat-leaf parsley leaves
- 1 cup (240g) crème fraîche
- 1 tablespoon finely grated lemon rind
- shredded lemon rind, to serve

1 Preheat oven to 180°C/350°F.

2 Rub 50g (1½ ounces) of the kale with 2 teaspoons of the oil. Place on an oven tray. Bake for 10 minutes or until crisp.

3 Meanwhile, heat remaining oil in a large saucepan over medium heat; cook onion and garlic, stirring, for 5 minutes or until softened.

4 Add stock and potato; bring to the boil. Reduce heat to low; simmer, covered, for 5 minutes.

5 Add broccoli; simmer, covered, for 6 minutes or until vegetables are tender.

6 Stir in remaining kale and parsley, cook for a further 1 minute or until just wilted. Remove soup from heat. Using a stick blender, carefully blend the soup until smooth. Season.

7 Combine crème fraîche and grated rind in a small bowl; season to taste.

8 Ladle soup into bowls; top with crème fraîche mixture, kale chips and shredded rind.

tips Sebago is a white-fleshed potato. You can use any white all-purpose non-waxy potato for this recipe. You can use chicken stock in place of vegetable stock, if you like. If using a jug blender or food processor to blend soup, stand it for 10 minutes to cool slightly before blending. The heat build-up can cause the lid to blow off. The soup, without crème fraîche, can be frozen for up to 3 months.

SMASHED POTATOES & KALE

PREP + COOK TIME 30 MINUTES **SERVES** 4

- **400g (12½ ounces) baby potatoes, halved if large**
- **½ teaspoon ground turmeric**
- **2 tablespoons olive oil**
- **60g (3 ounces) butter**
- **1 clove garlic, crushed**
- **400g (12½ ounces) green kale leaves, trimmed, torn**
- **2 tablespoons dukkah**
- **2 tablespoons small fresh mint leaves**

1 Place potatoes and turmeric in a medium saucepan with enough cold water to cover; bring to the boil. Cook for potatoes 15 minutes or until tender. Drain.

2 Heat oil and butter in same pan over medium-high heat; cook garlic and kale, stirring, for 5 minutes or until kale has wilted. Return potatoes to pan, using the back of a spoon, lightly smash each potato.

3 Add dukkah and mint leaves; toss to combine. Season.

KALE TARTS WITH MUHAMMARA

PREP + COOK TIME 45 MINUTES **SERVES** 6

- 6 sheets fillo pastry (120g)
- 2 tablespoons olive oil
- 2 tablespoons white chia seeds
- 4 green onions (scallions), chopped
- 80g (2½ ounces) baby kale leaves
- 400g (12½ ounces) canned chickpeas (garbanzo beans), drained, rinsed
- 1 clove garlic, crushed
- 150g (4½ ounces) ricotta, crumbled
- 125g (4 ounces) haloumi, chopped
- 2 teaspoons chopped fresh dill, plus extra, to serve

MUHAMMARA

- ¾ cup (180g) bottled roasted red capsicum (bell pepper), drained, reserving 1 tablespoon oil
- ½ cup (50g) toasted walnuts
- 1 tablespoon pomegranate molasses
- 1 tablespoon lemon juice

1 Preheat oven to 200°C/400°F. Lightly grease a 6-hole (¾-cup/180ml) texas muffin pan.

2 Layer fillo pastry sheets, brushing between each layer with 1 teaspoon oil and sprinkling with 1 teaspoon chia seeds. Cut pastry stack into six equal squares. Gently ease one stack into each muffin hole. Bake for 5 minutes. Reduce oven to 160°C/325°F.

3 Meanwhile, heat remaining oil in a large frying pan over medium heat; cook green onion, stirring for 3 minutes or until soft. Stir in kale, chickpeas and garlic; cook, stirring for 2 minutes or until kale has wilted. Transfer mixture to a large heatproof bowl; gently stir in ricotta, haloumi and dill until combined. Spoon kale mixture into pastry cases.

4 Bake for 20 minutes or until pastry is crisp and golden.

5 Meanwhile, make muhammara.

6 Serve tarts topped with muhammara and extra dill.

MUHAMMARA Process capsicum and reserved oil with walnuts, molasses and juice until smooth.

PROTEIN-RICH • HIGH IN CALCIUM

BRUSSELS SPROUTS, CAULIFLOWER & FARRO SALAD

PREP + COOK TIME 50 MINUTES SERVES 2

- **200g (6½ ounces) small brussels sprouts, trimmed, quartered**
- **200g (6½ ounces) cauliflower, cut into florets**
- **2 teaspoons olive oil**
- **1 tablespoon lemon juice**
- **2 teaspoons fresh lemon thyme leaves**
- **½ teaspoon ground sumac**
- **½ cup (100g) roasted farro**
- **1¼ cups (310ml) water**
- **2 shallots (50g), sliced thinly**
- **2 tablespoons chopped fresh flat-leaf parsley leaves**
- **1 tablespoon chopped fresh basil leaves**
- **1½ tablespoons white balsamic**
- **1 tablespoon macadamia oil**
- **¼ teaspoon salt**
- **40g (1½ ounces) baby kale leaves**
- **1 tablespoon pepitas (pumpkin seeds)**

1 Preheat oven to 200°C/400°F. Line an oven tray with baking paper.

2 Place sprouts and cauliflower on tray, drizzle with oil and juice; sprinkle with thyme and sumac. Roast for 20 minutes or until golden and tender.

3 Meanwhile, place farro and the water in a small saucepan; bring to the boil. Reduce heat to low; simmer, covered, for 30 minutes or until tender. Drain, rinse under cold water; drain well. Transfer farro to a medium bowl with shallot, parsley and basil; mix well.

4 Combine vinegar, oil and salt in a small bowl. Pour half the vinegar mixture over farro mixture; toss gently to combine.

5 Arrange sprouts, cauliflower, farro mixture and kale on a platter; sprinkle with seeds and drizzle with remaining vinegar mixture to serve.

tip Farro is a variety of wheat with a chewy texture and nutty flavour.

VEGAN • HIGH IN VITAMIN C • LOW GI

GLUTEN-FREE • EGG-FREE • DAIRY-FREE

KALE SALAD WITH CREAMY ZUCCHINI DRESSING

PREP + COOK TIME 25 MINUTES SERVES 6

- **1 cup (200g) red or white quinoa, rinsed, drained**
- **2 cups (500ml) water**
- **200g (6½ ounces) purple kale, trimmed, washed, sliced thinly**
- **1 large carrot (180g), unpeeled, grated coarsely**
- **1 cup (100g) walnuts, roasted, chopped coarsely**

ZUCCHINI DRESSING

- **2 small zucchini (180g), chopped coarsely**
- **1 large avocado (320g), chopped coarsely**
- **⅓ cup (35g) walnuts, roasted**
- **1 clove garlic, crushed**
- **2 tablespoons white wine vinegar**
- **2 tablespoons walnut oil**
- **2 tablespoons olive oil**

1 Make zucchini dressing.

2 Place quinoa and the water in a medium saucepan; bring to the boil. Reduce heat to low; simmer, covered, for 10 minutes or until tender. Drain; cool.

3 Place quinoa in a large bowl with kale, carrot, walnuts and dressing; toss gently to combine. Season to taste.

ZUCCHINI DRESSING

Process zucchini, avocado, walnuts, garlic and vinegar until smooth. With motor operating, gradually add both oils, drop by drop, then in a slow steady stream, until thick and creamy. Season to taste.

tips Quinoa and walnuts are packed with ample protein to make this a meal in itself for vegans and vegetarians, however, you could serve it as a side dish with grilled chicken, fish or a poached egg. It would also make a delicious filling for wraps or a sandwich.

serving suggestion Grilled chicken breast and lemon wedges.

WINTER VEGETABLE SAUTÉ WITH PROSCIUTTO & HAZELNUTS

PREP + COOK TIME 45 MINUTES SERVES 4

- 300g (9½ ounces) broccoli, cut into florets
- 300g (9½ ounces) baby brussels sprouts
- 320g (10 ounces) purple curly kale, trimmed, chopped coarsely
- 1 medium lemon (140g)
- 2 tablespoons olive oil
- 140g (4½ ounces) wholegrain sourdough bread, cut into pieces
- 75g (2½ ounces) thinly sliced prosciutto, chopped
- 1 large onion (200g), sliced thinly
- 4 cloves garlic, sliced thinly
- ⅓ cup (45g) hazelnuts, roasted, chopped coarsely
- ½ cup (125ml) chicken stock

1 Cook broccoli in a large saucepan of boiling water for 2 minutes or until just tender but still crisp. Drain immediately; refresh in iced water. Drain well. Repeat with sprouts, then kale.

2 Remove rind from lemon with a zester, into long thin strips (or grate finely). Squeeze juice from lemon; you will need 2 tablespoons juice.

3 Heat half the oil in a large frying pan over medium heat; cook bread pieces, stirring, for 5 minutes or until golden. Remove from pan.

4 Heat remaining oil in same pan over medium heat; cook prosciutto, stirring, for 2 minutes or until crisp. Remove with a slotted spoon; drain on paper towel. Reduce heat to medium-low; cook onion, stirring, for 10 minutes or until very soft. Add garlic; stir for 2 minutes. Add vegetables, rind and nuts; cook, stirring for 5 minutes until combined.

5 Increase heat to high, add stock and juice; simmer 1 minute or until vegetables are tender. Add prosciutto. Season to taste. Just before serving, scatter with toasted bread.

DAIRY-FREE • LOW CARB • HIGH-FIBRE

QUINOA CRUSTED KALE & FIG TART

PREP + COOK TIME 1 HOUR 30 MINUTES (+ REFRIGERATION) SERVES 6

- ¾ cup (150g) tri-coloured quinoa, rinsed, drained
- 1½ cups (120g) finely grated pecorino cheese
- 3 eggs
- 1 teaspoon sea salt flakes
- 1 tablespoon olive oil
- 1 clove garlic, crushed
- 3 cups (120g) firmly packed coarsely chopped kale
- ¼ cup (60ml) water
- 1 tablespoon dijon mustard
- ¾ cup (180ml) pouring cream
- 10 medium figs (600g)
- 1 cup (40g) loosely packed rocket (arugula) leaves
- ¼ cup (35g) roasted hazelnuts, halved

YOGHURT DRESSING

- ⅓ cup (95g) greek-style yoghurt
- 1 teaspoon raw honey
- 2 teaspoons chopped fresh tarragon
- ½ clove garlic, crushed

1 Grease an 11cm x 35cm (4½-inch x 14-inch) rectangular loose-based tart tin.

2 Cook quinoa in a large saucepan of boiling water for 12 minutes or until tender; drain well. Cool.

3 Process quinoa and half the pecorino until quinoa is finely chopped. Add 1 egg and half the salt; process until mixture forms a coarse dough. Press mixture evenly over base and sides of tart tin. Refrigerate for 30 minutes or until firm.

4 Meanwhile, preheat oven to 200°C/400°F.

5 Bake tart shell for 30 minutes or until golden. Remove from oven; reduce temperature to 180°C/350°F.

6 Meanwhile, heat oil in a medium frying pan over medium heat; cook garlic for 30 seconds. Add kale; cook, stirring, for 30 seconds. Add the water;

cook, covered, for 3 minutes. Remove from heat; stand, covered, for 1 minute. Cool; drain away any excess liquid.

7 Place kale mixture in a medium bowl with remaining eggs and salt, half the remaining pecorino, the mustard and cream; whisk to combine. Spread mixture into tart shell; sprinkle with remaining pecorino.

8 Bake tart for 30 minutes or until filling is set. Cut figs in half; place, cut-side up, on an oiled oven tray. Bake figs alongside tart, for 30 minutes or until just soft.

9 Make yoghurt dressing.

10 Serve tart topped with figs, rocket and hazelnuts; drizzle with dressing.

YOGHURT DRESSING

Combine ingredients in a small bowl; season to taste.

POACHED CHICKEN & KALE SALAD

PREP + COOK TIME 35 MINUTES SERVES 2

- ⅓ cup (65g) brown rice
- 1½ cups (375ml) water
- 250g (8 ounces) chicken breast fillets
- 125g (4 ounces) baby kale leaves
- 50g (1½ ounces) asparagus, halved lengthways
- 1 tablespoon olive oil
- 1 tablespoon red wine vinegar
- 2 teaspoons lemon juice
- 1 clove garlic, crushed
- 1 teaspoon dijon mustard
- ¼ teaspoon salt
- 2 tablespoons finely chopped fresh dill
- 3 green onions (scallions), sliced thinly
- 125g (4 ounces) cherry tomatoes, halved
- ½ medium avocado (125g), sliced thinly

1 Combine rice and the water in a small saucepan; bring to the boil. Boil, uncovered, for 30 minutes or until rice is tender; drain.

2 Meanwhile, half-fill a small saucepan with water; bring to the boil. Add chicken, return to the boil. Reduce heat; simmer, covered, for 10 minutes or until chicken is cooked through. Transfer chicken to a plate; cover, stand for 5 minutes, then shred coarsely.

3 Pour boiling water over kale and asparagus in a medium heatproof bowl; stand for 1 minute, drain. Refresh in a bowl of iced water; drain.

4 To make dressing, combine oil, vinegar, juice, garlic, mustard, salt and dill in a small bowl. Season with pepper.

5 Combine chicken, rice, kale, asparagus, onion, tomato and avocado in a serving bowl. Drizzle with dressing; toss gently to combine.

ROASTED KALE, SWEETCORN & CHICKPEA SALAD

PREP + COOK TIME 35 MINUTES SERVES 2

- **150g (4½ ounces) green kale leaves, trimmed, washed, torn into bite-size pieces**
- **1 teaspoon extra virgin olive oil**
- **pinch salt**
- **2 medium corn cobs (800g), husks and silk removed**
- **½ medium avocado (125g)**
- **½ cup (120g) rinsed, drained canned salt-reduced chickpeas (garbanzo beans)**
- **½ cup loosely packed fresh flat-leaf parsley leaves**
- **2 teaspoons extra virgin olive oil, extra**
- **1 tablespoon lemon juice**
- **1 clove garlic, crushed**
- **20g (¾ ounce) reduced-fat fetta, crumbled**
- **1 medium lemon (140g), cut into wedges**

1 Preheat oven to 200°C/400°F.

2 Place kale in a large bowl with oil and salt; using hands, massage leaves to coat well in oil and to soften. Arrange kale, in a single layer, on an oven tray. Roast for 20 minutes or until crisp.

3 Meanwhile, cook corn, on a heated oiled grill plate (or grill or barbecue), over medium-high heat, for 10 minutes or until lightly charred. Using a sharp knife, cut kernels from cob.

4 Using a spoon, scoop out pieces of avocado flesh. Combine kale, corn, chickpeas, avocado and parsley in a large bowl. Pour combined extra oil, juice and garlic over salad; toss gently to combine. Top salad with fetta; season to taste. Serve with lemon wedges.

LACTO - VEGETARIAN • IRON - RICH • HIGH - FIBRE

VEGIE & EGG POWER STACK

PREP + COOK TIME 40 MINUTES SERVES 4

- 1 medium kumara (orange sweet potato) (400g)
- 8 fresh shiitake mushrooms (140g), stems trimmed
- ¼ cup (60ml) olive oil
- 2 teaspoons chopped fresh rosemary
- 1 fresh long red chilli, seeded, chopped
- 2 tablespoons sunflower seeds
- 2 cups (80g) baby kale leaves
- ¼ cup (20g) finely grated parmesan
- 1 tablespoon white vinegar
- 8 eggs
- 3 green heirloom tomatoes (380g), sliced
- 4 baby target beetroot (beets) (80g), sliced thinly
- ½ cup baby micro cress

LEMON AÏOLI

- ½ cup (150ml) aïoli
- 2 tablespoons finely grated lemon rind
- 2 tablespoons lemon juice

1 Preheat oven to 200°C/400°F. Line an oven tray with baking paper.

2 Cut kumara into eight 5mm (¼-inch) thick rounds. Place on tray with mushrooms, 2 tablespoons of the oil, rosemary and chilli; toss to coat. Bake for 25 minutes or until kumara is tender.

3 Meanwhile, make lemon aïoli.

4 Heat remaining oil in a medium frying pan over medium heat; cook sunflower seeds, stirring, for 2 minutes or until toasted. Stir in kale, turn off heat; leave for the residual heat to wilt leaves. Add parmesan; season to taste.

5 To poach eggs, half-fill a large, deep-frying pan with water, add vinegar; bring to a gentle simmer. Break 1 egg into a cup. Using a wooden spoon, make a whirlpool in the water; slide egg into whirlpool. Repeat with 3 more eggs. Cook eggs for 3 minutes or until whites are set and the yolks are runny. Remove eggs with a slotted spoon; drain on a paper-towel-lined plate. Keep warm. Repeat poaching with remaining eggs.

6 Spoon 2 tablespoons of the aïoli onto each plate. Build two stacks on each plate with kumara, tomato, mushrooms then kale mixture. Top each stack with a poached egg, sliced beetroot and micro cress.

LEMON AÏOLI Combine ingredients in a small bowl; season to taste. Thin with a little warm water, if necessary.

GRILLED PORK WITH QUINOA & KALE SALAD

PREP + COOK TIME 30 MINUTES SERVES 2

- ⅓ cup (70g) black quinoa
- 1 small zucchini (90g), sliced into ribbons
- 1 medium carrot (120g), sliced into ribbons
- 1 small clove garlic, crushed
- 2 tablespoons lemon juice
- 1 tablespoon rice bran oil
- 2 x 125g (4 ounce) pork medallions
- 50g (1½ ounces) baby kale leaves
- 1 tablespoon fresh mint leaves
- 2 teaspoons pine nuts, toasted
- ½ lemon (70g), cut into wedges

1 Rinse and drain quinoa well. Cook quinoa in a small saucepan of boiling water for 10 minutes or until tender; drain. Refresh under cold water; drain.

2 Meanwhile, place zucchini, carrot, garlic, juice and half the oil in a medium bowl; toss gently to combine.

3 Heat remaining oil in a small frying pan over high heat; cook pork for 3 minutes each side or until browned both sides and just cooked through.

4 Add quinoa, kale, mint and nuts to zucchini mixture; toss gently to combine.

5 Serve pork with salad and lemon wedges.

HIGH · FIBRE · HIGH IN ANTIOXIDANTS · LOW GI · HIGH

HALOUMI, GRAPE & KALE FREEKEH SALAD

PREP + COOK TIME 30 MINUTES (+ COOLING) **SERVES** 4

- 1 cup (200g) cracked greenwheat freekeh
- 50g (1½ ounces) trimmed kale leaves
- ¼ cup loosely packed fresh basil leaves
- ½ cup (50g) walnuts
- 1 clove garlic, crushed
- ½ cup (40g) finely grated parmesan
- 2 tablespoons lemon juice
- ⅓ cup (80ml) olive oil
- 250g (8 ounces) haloumi, sliced
- 150g (4½ ounces) red seedless grapes, halved

1 Cook freekeh in a large saucepan of boiling salted water for 25 minutes or until just tender; drain well. Cool.

2 Process kale, basil leaves, walnuts, garlic, parmesan and juice until mixture forms a chunky paste. Stir in ¼ cup (60ml) of the oil; season to taste. Stir pesto through freekeh; set aside.

3 Heat remaining oil in a large frying pan over medium heat; cook haloumi slices for 1 minute each side or until golden brown.

4 Serve freekeh with haloumi and grapes.

GLOSSARY

ALMONDS flat, pointy-tipped nuts having a pitted brown shell enclosing a creamy white kernel which is covered by a brown skin.

ANCHOVIES small oily fish. Anchovy fillets are preserved and packed in oil or salt in small cans or jars, and are strong in flavour. Fresh anchovies are much milder in flavour.

AVOCADO the fruit of a family of large evergreen trees originating in Central and South America. Ripe avocados have soft, buttery flesh and a nutty flavour, and contain a high level of monounsaturated oil.

BASIL used extensively in Italian dishes and one of the main ingredients in pesto.

BEAN SPROUTS tender new growths of assorted beans and seeds germinated for consumption as sprouts.

BREAD
pitta also known as lebanese bread. This wheat-flour pocket bread is sold in large, flat pieces that separate into two thin rounds.
sourdough a low-risen bread with a dense centre and crisp crust; made from a yeast starter culture used to make the previous loaf of bread. May or may not have a sour flavour.

BROCCOLI belongs to the cabbage family and consists of tiny, tightly clustered flower buds on thick, fleshy stalks. It comes in green and purple varieties (the purple changes to green as it is cooked). The stalks, which are delicately flavoured and tender once the tough skin has been peeled away, can be used in the same way as the flower heads.

BRUISING a cooking term to describe the slight crushing given to aromatic ingredients, particularly garlic and herbs, with the flat side of a heavy knife or cleaver to release flavour and aroma.

BUTTER use salted or unsalted (sweet) butter; 125g (4 ounces) is equal to one stick of butter.

BUTTERMILK originally the term given to the slightly sour liquid left after butter was churned from cream, today it is made from no-fat or low-fat milk to which specific bacterial cultures have been added. Despite its name, it is actually low in fat.

CAPSICUM (BELL PEPPER) also called pepper. Comes in many colours: red, green, yellow, orange and purplish-black. Be sure to discard seeds and membranes before use.

CARDAMOM a spice native to India; can be purchased in pod, seed or ground form. Has a distinctive aromatic, sweetly rich flavour and is one of the world's most expensive spices.

CASHEWS plump, kidney-shaped, golden-brown nuts having a distinctive sweet, buttery flavour and containing about 48% fat.

CHEESE
blue mould-treated cheeses mottled with blue veining. Varieties include firm and crumbly stilton types and mild, creamy brie-like cheeses.
fetta Greek in origin; a crumbly textured goat- or sheep-milk cheese having a sharp, salty taste. Ripened and stored in salted whey.
haloumi a firm, cream-coloured sheep-milk cheese matured in brine; haloumi can be grilled or fried, briefly, without breaking down. Should be eaten while still warm as it becomes tough and rubbery on cooling.
parmesan also called parmigiano; is a hard, grainy cow-milk cheese originating in Italy. Reggiano is the best variety.
pecorino hard, white to pale-yellow in colour. If you can't find it, use parmesan instead.

ricotta a soft, sweet, moist, white cow-milk cheese with a low fat content (8.5 %) and a slightly grainy texture. The name roughly translates as "cooked again" and refers to ricotta's manufacture from a whey that is itself a by-product of other cheese making.

CHIA SEEDS contain protein and all the essential amino acids and a wealth of vitamins, minerals and antioxidants, as well as being fibre-rich.

CHICKPEAS (GARBANZO BEANS) also called hummus or channa; an irregularly round, sandy-coloured legume used extensively in Mediterranean, Indian and Hispanic cooking.

CHICKEN, BREAST FILLET breast halved, skinned and boned.

CHILLI use rubber gloves when seeding and chopping fresh chillies as they can burn your skin.

cayenne pepper a thin-fleshed, long, extremely hot dried red chilli, usually purchased ground.

flakes, dried deep-red, dehydrated chilli slices and whole seeds.

long red available both fresh and dried; a generic term used for any moderately hot, long, thin chilli (about 6cm to 8cm long).

powder the Asian variety is the hottest, made from dried ground thai chillies; can be used instead of fresh in the proportion of ½ teaspoon chilli powder to 1 medium fresh red chilli.

thai (serrano) also known as "scuds"; tiny, very hot and bright red in colour.

COCONUT

cream obtained commercially from the first pressing of the coconut flesh alone, without the addition of water.

milk not the liquid inside the fruit (coconut water), but the diluted liquid from the second pressing of the white flesh of a mature coconut. Available in cans and cartons at most supermarkets.

CORIANDER (CILANTRO) also called pak chee or chinese parsley; bright-green-leafed herb with both pungent aroma and taste. Both the stems and roots of coriander are used in Thai cooking: wash well before chopping. Is also available ground or as seeds; these should not be substituted for fresh.

CREAM

pouring also called pure or fresh cream. It has no additives and contains a minimum fat content of 35%.

thick (double) a dolloping cream with a minimum fat content of 45%.

thickened (heavy) a whipping cream containing thickener. Minimum fat content 35%.

CRÈME FRAÎCHE mature fermented cream with a slightly tangy, nutty flavour and velvety texture. Used in savoury and sweet dishes. Minimum fat content 35%.

CUCUMBER, LEBANESE short, slender and thin-skinned. Probably the most popular variety because of its tender, edible skin, tiny, yielding seeds, and sweet, fresh and flavoursome taste.

CUMIN also known as zeera or comino; resembling caraway in size, cumin is the dried seed of a plant related to the parsley family. Black cumin seeds are smaller than standard cumin, and dark brown rather than true black.

DILL also known as dill weed; used fresh or dried, in seed form or ground. Its frond-like fresh leaves are grassier and more subtle than the dried version or the seeds.

DUKKAH an Egyptian specialty spice mixture made up of roasted nuts, seeds and an array of aromatic spices.

EGGS we use large chicken eggs weighing an average of 60g unless stated otherwise in the recipes in this book.

FENNEL also known as finocchio or anise; a white to very pale green-white, firm, crisp, roundish vegetable about 8-12cm in diameter. The bulb has a slightly sweet, anise flavour but the leaves have a much stronger taste.

FLAT-LEAF PARSLEY also known as continental parsley or italian parsley.

FREEKEH also known as farek, young green wheat that has been toasted and cracked.

FILLO PASTRY paper-thin sheets of raw pastry; brush each sheet with oil or melted butter, stack in layers, then cut and fold as directed.

GARAM MASALA spice mix based on varying proportions of cardamom, cinnamon, cloves, coriander, fennel and cumin, roasted and ground together.

GINGER, FRESH also called green or root ginger; the thick gnarled root of a tropical plant. Can be kept, peeled, covered with dry sherry in a jar and refrigerated, or frozen in an airtight container. Ground ginger cannot be substituted for fresh ginger.

GLUTEN is a combination of two proteins found in wheat (including spelt), rye, barley and oats. When liquid is added to the flour, these two proteins bind to become gluten. Gluten gives elasticity to dough, helping it rise and keep its shape; it also gives the final product a chewy texture.

HAZELNUTS also known as filberts; plump, grape-sized, rich, sweet nut having a brown skin that is removed by rubbing heated nuts together vigorously in a tea-towel.

HONEY the variety sold in a squeezable container is not suitable for the recipes in this book.

KALE is a type of leafy cabbage, rich in nutrients and vitamins. Leaf colours can range from green to violet.

KUMARA the Polynesian name of an orange-fleshed sweet potato often confused with yam.

LABNE is yoghurt that has been strained to remove its whey, resulting in a thicker consistency than unstrained yoghurt, while preserving yoghurt's distinctive, sour taste.

LEEKS a member of the onion family, the leek resembles a green onion but is much larger and more subtle in flavour.

LINSEEDS also known as flaxseeds, they are the richest plant source of omega 3 fats, which are essential for a healthy brain, heart, joints and immune system.

MACADAMIAS native to Australia; fairly large, slightly soft, buttery rich nut. Used to make oil and macadamia butter; equally good in salads or cakes and pastries; delicious eaten on their own. Should always be stored in the fridge to prevent their high oil content turning them rancid.

MAYONNAISE, WHOLE-EGG commercial mayonnaise of high quality made with whole eggs and labelled as such; some prepared mayonnaises substitute emulsifiers such as food starch, cellulose gel or other thickeners to achieve the same thick and creamy consistency but never achieve the same rich flavour. Must be refrigerated once opened.

MUSHROOMS, SHIITAKE also known as chinese black, or golden oak mushrooms; large and meaty and have the earthiness and taste of wild mushrooms.

MUSTARD, DIJON also called french. Pale brown, creamy, distinctively flavoured, fairly mild French mustard.

OIL

cooking spray we use a cholesterol-free cooking spray made from canola oil.

hazelnut oil see *Hazelnuts*

macadamia oil see *Macadamias*

olive made from ripened olives; "light" refers to taste not fat levels.

peanut pressed from ground peanuts; commonly used oil in Asian cooking because of its high smoke point (capacity to handle high heat without burning).

rice bran is extracted from the germ and inner husk of the rice grain; has a mild, slightly nutty, flavour. Its high smoke point means it's suitable for high-temperature cooking methods.

sesame made from roasted, crushed, white sesame seeds; a flavouring rather than a cooking medium.

vegetable any of a number of oils sourced from plant rather than animal fats.

OREGANO

a herb; has a woody stalk and clumps of tiny, dark-green leaves. Has a pungent, peppery flavour.

ONIONS

brown and white are interchangeable, however, white onions have a more pungent flesh.

green (scallions) also known, incorrectly, as shallots; an immature onion picked before the bulb has formed, having a long, bright-green edible stalk.

red also known as spanish, red spanish or bermuda onion; a sweet-flavoured, large, purple-red onion.

shallots also called french shallots, golden shallots or eschalots. Small and elongated, with a brown skin, they grow in tight clusters similar to garlic.

PAPRIKA

ground, dried, sweet red capsicum (bell pepper); there are many types available, including sweet, hot, mild and smoked.

PEPITAS (PUMPKIN SEEDS)

are the pale green kernels of dried pumpkin seeds; they can be bought plain or salted.

PINE NUTS

also known as pignoli; not a nut but a small, cream-coloured kernel from pine cones.

POMEGRANATE MOLASSES

not to be confused with pomegranate syrup or grenadine (used in cocktails); pomegranate molasses is thicker, browner, and more concentrated in flavour — tart and sharp, slightly sweet and fruity. Buy from Middle Eastern food stores or specialty food shops.

PROSCIUTTO

a kind of unsmoked Italian ham; salted, air-cured and aged, it is usually eaten uncooked. There are many styles of prosciutto, one of the best being Parma ham, from Italy's Emilia Romagna region, traditionally lightly salted, dried then eaten raw.

QUINOA

pronounced keen-wa; is a gluten-free grain. It has a delicate, slightly nutty taste and chewy texture.

RICE

brown retains the high-fibre, nutritious bran coating that's removed from white rice when hulled. It takes longer to cook than white rice and has a chewier texture. Once cooked, the long grains stay separate, while the short grains are soft and stickier.

microwave milled, cooked then dried rice. Pre-cooked rice is more porous, so steam can penetrate the grain and rehydrate it in a short time.

ROCKET (ARUGULA)

also called rugula and rucola; peppery green leaf eaten raw in salads or used in cooking.

ROSEMARY

pungent herb with long, thin pointy leaves; use large and small sprigs, and the leaves are usually chopped finely.

SESAME SEEDS black and white are the most common of this small oval seed. Roast the seeds in a heavy-based frying pan over low heat.

SILVER BEET also called swiss chard; mistakenly called spinach.

SOPRESSA a salami from the north of Italy, can be found in both mild and chilli-flavoured varieties. If you can't find it easily, you can use any hot salami, but the taste won't be exactly the same.

SOY SAUCE also known as sieu; made from fermented soybeans. Several variations are available in supermarkets and Asian food stores; we use Japanese soy sauce unless indicated otherwise.

SPINACH also known as english spinach and incorrectly, silver beet. Baby spinach leaves are best eaten raw in salads; the larger leaves should be added last to soups, stews and stir-fries, and should be cooked until barely wilted.

SUMAC a purple-red, astringent spice ground from berries growing on shrubs that flourish wild around the Mediterranean; adds a tart, lemony flavour to dips and dressings and goes well with barbecued meat. Can be found in Middle Eastern food stores.

SUNFLOWER SEEDS grey-green, slightly soft, oily kernels; a nutritious snack.

TAMARI similar to but thicker than japanese soy; very dark in colour with a distinctively mellow flavour. Good used as a dipping sauce or for basting.

TAMARIND the tamarind tree produces clusters of hairy brown pods, each of which is filled with seeds and a viscous pulp, that are dried and pressed into the blocks of tamarind found in Asian food shops. Gives a sweet-sour, slightly astringent taste to marinades, pastes, sauces and dressings.

TAMARIND PASTE also called concentrate; the commercial result of the distillation of tamarind juice into a condensed, compacted paste.

TOMATOES

canned whole peeled tomatoes in natural juices; available crushed, chopped or diced, sometimes unsalted or reduced salt. Use undrained.

cherry also known as tiny tim or tom thumb tomatoes; small and round.

paste triple-concentrated tomato puree used to flavour soups, stews, sauces and casseroles.

TURMERIC also called kamin; is a rhizome related to galangal and ginger. Must be grated or pounded to release its flavour. Known for the golden colour it imparts, fresh turmeric can be substituted with the more commonly found dried powder.

VINEGAR

red wine based on fermented red wine.

white made from spirit of cane sugar.

white balsamic (vinegar or condiment) is a clear and lighter version of balsamic vinegar; it has a fresh, sweet clean taste.

white wine made from a blend of white wines.

WALNUTS as well as being a good source of fibre and healthy oils, nuts contain a range of vitamins, minerals and other beneficial plant components called phytochemicals. Walnuts contain the beneficial omega-3 fatty acids.

YOGHURT, GREEK-STYLE plain yoghurt strained in a cloth (muslin) to remove the whey and to give it a creamy consistency.

ZUCCHINI also called courgette; a small, pale- or dark-green or yellow vegetable belonging to the squash family.

CONVERSION CHART

MEASURES

One Australian metric measuring cup holds approximately 250ml; one Australian metric tablespoon holds 20ml; one Australian metric teaspoon holds 5ml.

The difference between one country's measuring cups and another's is within a two- or three-teaspoon variance, and will not affect your cooking results. North America, New Zealand and the United Kingdom use a 15ml tablespoon.

All cup and spoon measurements are level. The most accurate way of measuring dry ingredients is to weigh them. When measuring liquids, use a clear glass or plastic jug with the metric markings.

The imperial measurements used in these recipes are approximate only. Measurements for cake pans are approximate only. Using same-shaped cake pans of a similar size should not affect the outcome of your baking. We measure the inside top of the cake pan to determine sizes.

We use large eggs with an average weight of 60g.

DRY MEASURES

METRIC	IMPERIAL
15G	½OZ
30G	1OZ
60G	2OZ
90G	3OZ
125G	4OZ (¼LB)
155G	5OZ
185G	6OZ
220G	7OZ
250G	8OZ (½LB)
280G	9OZ
315G	10OZ
345G	11OZ
375G	12OZ (¾LB)
410G	13OZ
440G	14OZ
470G	15OZ
500G	16OZ (1LB)
750G	24OZ (1½LB)
1KG	32OZ (2LB)

LIQUID MEASURES

METRIC	IMPERIAL
30ML	1 FLUID OZ
60ML	2 FLUID OZ
100ML	3 FLUID OZ
125ML	4 FLUID OZ
150ML	5 FLUID OZ
190ML	6 FLUID OZ
250ML	8 FLUID OZ
300ML	10 FLUID OZ
500ML	16 FLUID OZ
600ML	20 FLUID OZ
1000ML (1 LITRE)	1¾ PINTS

LENGTH MEASURES

METRIC	IMPERIAL
3MM	⅛IN
6MM	¼IN
1CM	½IN
2CM	¾IN
2.5CM	1IN
5CM	2IN
6CM	2½IN
8CM	3IN
10CM	4IN
13CM	5IN
15CM	6IN
18CM	7IN
20CM	8IN
22CM	9IN
25CM	10IN
28CM	11IN
30CM	12IN (1FT)

OVEN TEMPERATURES

The oven temperatures in this book are for conventional ovens; if you have a fan-forced oven, decrease the temperature by 10-20 degrees.

	°C (CELSIUS)	°F (FAHRENHEIT)
VERY SLOW	120	250
SLOW	150	300
MODERATELY SLOW	160	325
MODERATE	180	350
MODERATELY HOT	200	400
HOT	220	425
VERY HOT	240	475

INDEX

PUBLISHED IN 2016 BY BAUER MEDIA BOOKS, AUSTRALIA.
BAUER MEDIA BOOKS IS A DIVISION OF BAUER MEDIA PTY LTD.

BAUER MEDIA BOOKS

PUBLISHER
JO RUNCIMAN

EDITORIAL & FOOD DIRECTOR
PAMELA CLARK

DIRECTOR OF SALES, MARKETING & RIGHTS
BRIAN CEARNES

CREATIVE DIRECTOR
HANNAH BLACKMORE

SENIOR EDITOR
STEPHANIE KISTNER

DESIGNER
JEANNEL CUNANAN

JUNIOR EDITOR
AMANDA LEES

FOOD EDITOR
REBECCA MELI

OPERATIONS MANAGER
DAVID SCOTTO

COVER PHOTOGRAPHER
JAMES MOFFATT

STYLIST
ARUM SHIM

PRINTED IN CHINA
BY C&C OFFSET PRINTING

TITLE: SUPER KALE / PAMELA CLARK.
ISBN: 9781742458540 (HARDBACK)
NOTES: INCLUDES INDEX.
SUBJECTS: COOKING (KALE)
 COOKING (GREENS). NATURAL FOODS.
OTHER CREATORS/CONTRIBUTORS:
 CLARK, PAMELA (FOOD DIRECTOR)
DEWEY NUMBER: 641.65347

© BAUER MEDIA PTY LIMITED 2016
ABN 18 053 273 546

PUBLISHED BY BAUER MEDIA BOOKS,
A DIVISION OF BAUER MEDIA PTY LTD,
54 PARK ST, SYDNEY; GPO BOX 4088,
SYDNEY, NSW 2001, AUSTRALIA
PH +61 2 9282 8618; FAX +61 2 9126 3702
WWW.AWWCOOKBOOKS.COM.AU

ORDER BOOKS
PHONE 136 116 (WITHIN AUSTRALIA)

OR ORDER ONLINE AT
WWW.AWWCOOKBOOKS.COM.AU

SEND RECIPE ENQUIRIES TO
RECIPEENQUIRIES@BAUER-MEDIA.COM.AU